BRITAIN IN OLD PHOTOGRAPHS

SOUTHPORT

JACK SMITH

Budding BOOKS

A Budding Book

This book was first published in 1995 by
Sutton Publishing Limited
Phoenix Mill · Thrupp · Stroud
Gloucestershire · GL5 2BU

This edition first published in 2001 by
Budding Books, an imprint of
Sutton Publishing Limited

British Library Cataloguing in Publication Data.
A catalogue record for this book is available from the British Library.

ISBN 1 84015 220 6

Typeset in 9/10 Sabon.
Typesetting and origination by
Sutton Publishing Limited.
Printed and bound in Great Britain by
J.H. Haynes & Co. Ltd, Sparkford.

The bowling greens on the foreshore, 1918.

Contents

Introduction

As a child in the 1940s, apart from the forty-five minute bus ride, my earliest recollections of trips to Southport with my parents are of carefree hours spent with bucket and spade on the Children's Beach, on swings and slides at the Peter Pan Playground, or of being taken for a row on the Marine Lake. Sometimes I was lucky enough to ride on a miniature railway where I would try to get as close as I could to the steam engine. Occasionally I was allowed to sail my model yacht on the pond in Princes Park – I remember how jealous I used to feel of some of the larger, expensive boats being sailed by other children's fathers. . . . And as a special treat I might get taken to the fairground, or Pleasureland as it is called. But there were other, much less happy times when I would have to be on my best behaviour, tagging along behind my parents as they browsed in the shops in and around Lord Street. There was a café which we always visited, in the present Wayfarers Arcade in Lord Street; its atmosphere was so decorous – all you could hear was the clinking of teaspoons in cups and saucers and the quiet tones of hushed conversations. I was always being told to be quiet. Even in the

Mr William Mellors, *c.* 1900. He married Elizabeth Dean, daughter of Mr Dean, founder of a confectioners business. The firm eventually became Mellors Confectioners which celebrated its 150th anniversary in 1990. The company now has several retail outlets in the area.

1990s, half a century later, that arcade still holds special significance for me.

Perhaps best known as a genteel resort, famous for its shopping, the present town of Southport has an interesting history going back some two hundred years. Before then, the area was covered by sand dunes, the tide coming in as far as Lord Street, and at high tide even further – as far as Chapel Street, now over half a mile from the sea. The district was originally called North Meols from the Scandinavian name meaning 'sand hill'. Established in the thirteenth century, North Meols lay on a strip of land with the sea to the west and a large marsh and lake, called Martin Mere, to the east. This mere was fed from inland streams and was partially tidal. Some of the earliest evidence of habitation comes from the finds of prehistoric canoes unearthed in the area near the former mere.

Thousands of years before this a great primeval forest, stretching from the River Ribble estuary to the north and the River Mersey in the south, covered the coast hereabouts, and traces of it can at times be found on the beaches. A legend about Martin Mere even suggests that it was associated with stories of King Arthur, but today it is best known for its bird sanctuary.

The main settlement in North Meols was Churchtown, with its church dedicated to St Cuthbert whose remains were allegedly placed to rest here some time during the ninth century when the monks were forced to carry away the bones of their saint from their original resting place to avoid seizure or destruction by Viking raiders. The present church is reputedly built on the site of the actual monks' encampment.

Now 2 miles or so from the coast, it is hard to imagine that once a river connected the village to the sea and that vessels sailed right to Churchtown and tied up at the 'otter pool'. Today the boating lake in the Botanic Gardens at Churchtown follows the line of the old river. West of Churchtown two hundred years ago the ground was sandy, with a few cottages scattered among the dunes. Their inhabitants were fishermen, shrimpers and cockle gatherers, called 'sandgrounders', and they lived in an area known then as South Hawes, later to have quite an important change of name. Nor was fishing their only means of making a livelihood in those days. The dangerous channels off the coast led to many shipwrecks and there were some who earned a living by stealing from the wrecks or from smuggling.

The origin of modern Southport has become something of a legend, with its variations of course, but the man responsible appears to have been William 'Duke' Sutton. Sutton was landlord of the Churchtown pub, The Black Bull, in the 1790s. In those days Churchtown was frequented in the summer months by visitors coming to spend time on the beach and bathe, but they had to travel the 2 miles from the village to the sea. An enterprising man, Sutton gathered driftwood and built a bathing hut close to the beach so that the visitors could change in comfort. Sutton was much ridiculed for his 'hut', and it was nicknamed 'Duke's Folly'. The year was 1792 and the location of the 'Folly' was the southern end of the present Lord Street, with its junction with Lord Street West, close to the River Nile.

Despite its crudeness, 'Duke's Folly' proved popular, was improved and needed to be rebuilt owing to weather damage sustained over the winter. A few cottages were constructed close to the 'Folly' and in 1798 Sutton himself built a cottage alongside the original bathing hut. With the resort's increasing popularity Sutton arranged for a ship-load of building material to be brought from Liverpool to construct a hotel, a little inland from the original site. The story goes that this cargo was unloaded at the 'South Port', this name being used at a party where William Sutton and his friends were celebrating in the old 'Folly'. It is said that an official christening of the hut walls was carried out also, naming the place South Port in North Meols. More rows of cottages were built, close to the new hotel, and between 1805 and 1840 the town grew rapidly. In 1835 a sea wall was constructed with a promenade behind it; another two hotels and the

Victorian Baths were also erected. In 1840, Lord Street was developing with several shops and houses already built. Expansion was such that by 1848 a board of commissioners was established, the first town council.

The earliest rail service into Southport, as it had now become, started up in 1840 when a line from Liverpool opened, followed seven years later by one from Manchester. The railways certainly made a difference to the town, not only because more people came to live there but because the connections brought a large increase in the numbers of visitors and holiday-makers. The 1860s saw the town council setting up parks and gardens, and by the mid-1870s the population had reached 18,000. A railway from Preston was opened in 1882, and a second line from Liverpool via Ainsdale was completed in 1884. The foreshore was purchased from the lord of the manor in 1885 and schemes to reclaim that area put under way. It is hard to envisage that at this time the beach extended from the promenade, the only man-made structure being the pier, built in 1860, which was 1,200 yards long and extended to 1,465 yards in 1867. From the pier head steamers sailed to some fifteen ports, from Barrow in Furness to the north to several Welsh destinations to the south. The last passenger steamer left the pier in 1923 en route to Blackpool – the silting up of the channels forced the ship owners to put an end to the sailings.

A huge amount of reclamation work has gone on along the foreshore; both North and South Marine lakes had been constructed by 1895 and the extensive Kings Gardens laid out along the promenade together with a fairground. In 1913 land for the municipal golf course was reclaimed while the fairground moved to its present site at Pleasureland in 1922 followed by the construction of the new Sea Bathing Lake in 1928. The beach was used extensively for motor car racing in the 1920s and '30s. Indeed, Southport's sporting associations are numerous: they range from curling in the 'glaciarium', to sand yacht racing, croquet, horse racing (immortalized by Red Rum who lives and trains here), and, of course, golf. There are nine courses here, six maintained to championship standard. Then there are the water sports: yachting, powerboat racing, paragliding, rowing, water skiing – the list is almost endless.

Having celebrated its bicentenary in 1992, modern Southport faces many challenges owing to its Victorian beginnings; of these, changes and structural renewals predominate, as they have for many years. One such major undertaking was the replacement of the Opera House by the Garrick Theatre, itself superseded by Southport Theatre in the 1970s. The three railway stations are now reduced to one. There was further reclamation of the foreshore with the building of the marine drive in the 1960s. Now, in the 1990s, alongside the pier, the Marine Parade Bridge, badly in need of repair to its ironwork, has been closed for some time. The pier itself is also suffering from the ravages of time, and teeters on the brink of demolition. Essential parts of the history of Southport's foreshore, it is to be hoped that both pier and bridge will be restored to their former glory, perhaps as part of a Project 2000 scheme.

A Lancashire resort until 1974, Southport is now in the Metropolitan Borough of Sefton, Merseyside, but the controversy over whether to remain in Merseyside or return to Lancashire continues, as do the problems of funding and organizing improvements to road and rail systems, conservation and preservation projects. All this needs to be solved so that Southport can continue to provide its wealth of amenities. The parks and gardens of Southport are as essential as its shops and stores; its sporting facilities are legendary. Because of this wide range of facilities Southport will continue to attract the holiday-maker, day-tripper, shopper and sports enthusiast, as well as the thousands who flock to the annual Southport Flower Show, into the millennium. The town's motto *Salus populi lex supremo est*, shortened to *Salus populi* ('The Welfare of the People'), is still very relevant today.

Jack Smith, June 1995

Section One

BEACH & PIER

Donkey rides on the sands, c. *1910. They are just as popular today as they were then.*

Some of the local ladies 'riddling' for shellfish on the beach at low tide, *c.* 1890. Their baskets were made at Mawdesley, a village 8 miles inland and famous for its basketmaking. The 'sandgrounders' of North Meols earned their living from fishing, shrimping and cockling, taking their catches to the towns of Ormskirk and Preston to be sold in the markets, or for resale further afield.

Menfolk using wooden rakes to find cockles in the wet sand, *c.* 1925. Sieves and baskets were the other 'tools of the trade'.

A group of 'shrimpers' coming along the pier after their boats were tied up. Note the 'harness' type of carrier for the bags of shrimp they have caught.

Fishing boats tied up at the end of the pier, *c.* 1900. The pier head was also used by steamers carrying trippers from Southport to the Lake District or ports in North Wales.

A frozen sea in early 1895 trapped the fishing boats for some time and caused damage to some of them. The fishermen risked life and limb to try and clear a channel, at times riding the ice floes armed with long poles and boat hooks. This cold spell lasted several weeks.

This interesting etching, *c.* 1890, shows the pier entrance in the foreground (admission 2*d*). Construction of the pier began on 14 August 1859 when the first pile was driven. A year later, in August 1860, it was opened with great celebration, processions, banquets, illuminations and fireworks heralding the new attraction. At the opening ceremony the company chairman paid tribute to Mr Boothroyd, whose idea it had been to build Southport a pier.

Creation of the South Marine Lake, to the left of the pier, was first mooted in 1886; construction of the north lake, to the right of the pier, was started in 1891. The bridge carrying the road along Marine Drive, to the right of the picture, was first used to launch the town lifeboat, which was frequently called out.

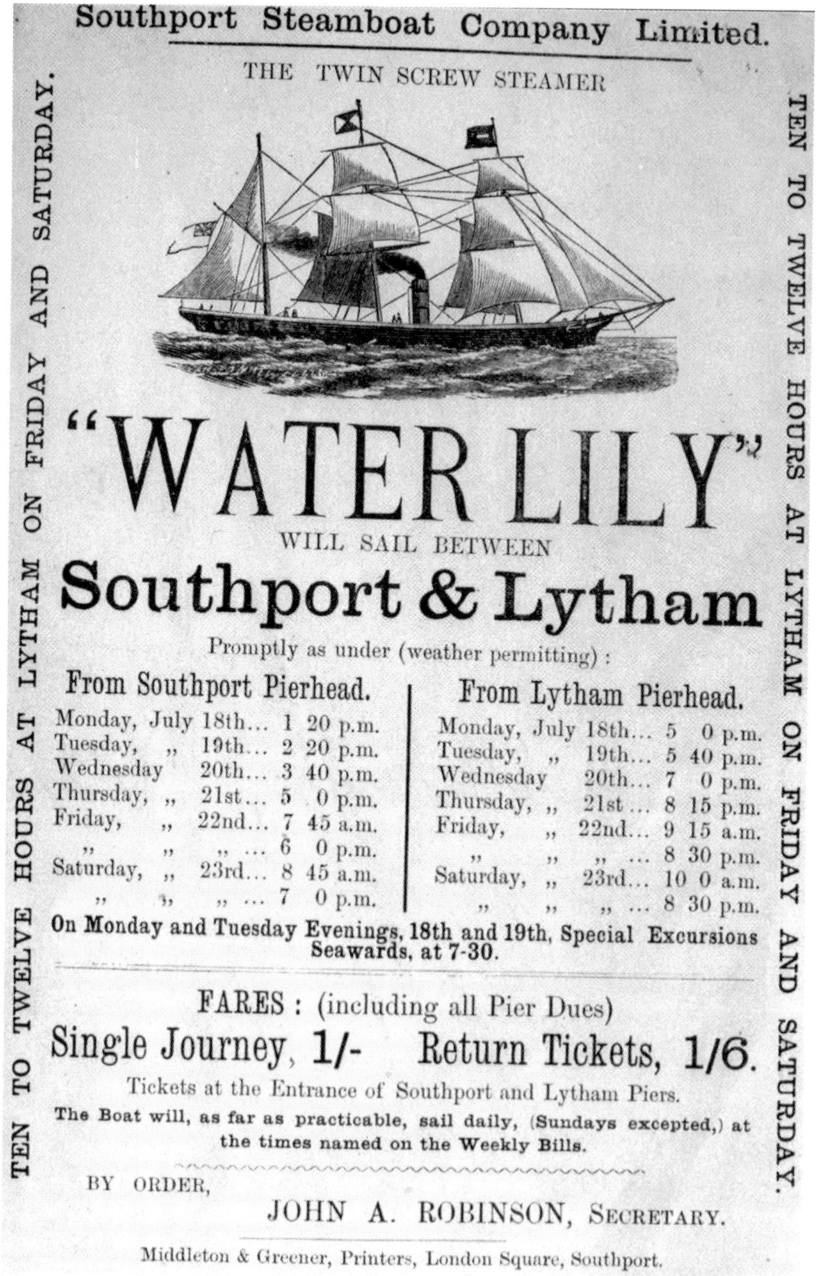

A poster advertising sailings from the end of the pier, probably dating from the 1880s. Steamers had been sailing in and out of Southport since the mid-1830s, when the Preston, Lytham and Southport Steam Navigation Company conveyed passengers to fifteen ports along the north-west coast.

Passengers on deck, suitably dressed for the bracing air of the sea trip. Sailings from the end of the pier ended in the 1920s because of the silting up of the channels.

Children paddling in the South Marine Lake in the 1890s, and hardly a knee in sight let alone a bathing costume. In the distance is part of the aerial cableway tower.

Donkey rides on the sands, *c.* 1900. Notice what seems to be the early fairground in the distance.

How the riders' clothing dates this snapshot! You don't see many men sporting bowler hats nowadays – and certainly not on the beach.

Beach scene to the south side of the pier at the turn of the century. Apart from the 'overdressed' people, here is an interesting and rare view of the cableway tower. The cableway carried passengers over the South Marine Lake in gondolas.

A beach ice cream seller with caped and capped children enjoying their purchases, early 1900s. Ice cream was scooped out of the tub and served in glasses, which stand ready on the stall.

Watching the pier divers was a popular pastime at the turn of the century. Here 'Professor' Osborne (they all had this title) is about to dive off the roof of Thoms Tea House at the end of the pier. Thoms had another tea establishment at 291 Lord Street.

Another diver was 'Professor' Powsey, here seen in mid-air, having climbed to the top of a tall platform before his dive. Mr Powsey was a diver for over twenty years, last diving at the age of seventy-three. He died in 1956 aged eighty-nine.

A favourite pastime while on the pier was picture postcard writing. The card above has two small pictures of Southport superimposed on a washtub and clothes basket – no washing machines then. The bottom card shows five views of the town. Both date from the late 1930s.

Enjoying the sunshine and sea breeze, visitors at the end of the pier watch the yachts or fishermen, 1950s. Most of them will have travelled the length of the pier by a special train, although the more energetic will have chosen to walk.

Making sandpies, 1930s. I don't suppose this popular pastime will ever go out of fashion. At least on Southport Beach castles stood longer, for the tide rarely came all the way up to the sea wall.

The tide right up to the wall, and providing a grand spectacle. Here a crowd are dodging the waves. Behind them stands the Promenade, with, centre, the Convalescent Hospital, opened by the 5th Earl of Derby in 1883. It was built from surplus monies raised for the Lancashire Cotton Relief Fund.

Happy children, and some not too sure, riding beach ponies in the late 1940s. The location is the Children's Beach, an area very popular with visitors.

Ex-military vehicles providing rides along the beach during the late 1940s. Here, bottom right, one is about to set off down to Ainsdale and back. These open-top vehicles were also used around the town on some routes at this time. Another ex-military vehicle can be seen in the distance. This is a DUKW, which also was used for rides.

A beach ride vehicle loading up with passengers. This was either a Thornycroft or a Bedford.

The Children's Beach from the Pier Pavilion, looking across the Marine Parade Bridge which spans the Marine Lake. Peter Pan's Playground can just be seen to the left-hand side in the distance. Sadly, the bridge is now in a poor state of repair and closed to the public.

What an unusual sight on an English beach! The animals here were from a visiting circus which came to town in the 1950s.

Looking across the promenade to the Marine Parade, with the pier to the left. The Floral Hall Gardens are to the front right, Marine Lake and Children's Beach in the distance. Here is a wealth of interesting detail: Ed Harper's band is playing at the Floral Hall; admission to the Floral Hall Gardens is Adult 1*s*, Child 0*s* 6*d*; a Blundells coach (295 KTU) is unloading day visitors; and at the Pier Casino, Harry Hudson is starring in *Let's have a Party*. Parking appears to be free. . . . The date can be established from the poster to the lower right, for the 1961 'English Rose' competition. Additionally, the floral advertisement on the lawn refers to the Southport Flower Show of 1962.

Families packing the popular Children's Beach sometime in the late 1950s or early 1960s. The scene could be from the 1990s, except that there would be rather more flesh on show! Everybody seems to be so typically reserved and covered up, even though it is a lovely day. Where are the shorts? Not a pair in sight, although a couple of men are 'topless', with trousers still on, though. There are even some men wearing suits. . . . In the background is the North Marine Lake with the Promenade behind.

The Marine Drive, beach and pier in the late 1940s, close to Pleasureland. Parents tried hard to keep their children away from its attractions as the roundabouts, slides and sideshows seemed to eat up money, so in many cases it was to the beach with bat and ball and a picnic by the car.

This picture is taken from a 'Passenger Certificate' certifying that the bearer had flown at over 1,000 feet. It was given to passengers as a souvenir on the Southport to Blackpool flight. The company used the beach for take-off and landing. The 'G' stands for Giro, short for Norman Giroux, pilot and later company boss.

Section Two

PROMENADE & FORESHORE

Southport's first sea wall and Promenade, built during the 1840s, depicted here in 1850 in a sketch by E. Vernon. To the left is the Victoria Baths, built in 1839, and enlarged in 1871. Today it is hard to imagine that the sea once came up to the Promenade, for so much of the foreshore area has been reclaimed.

The magnificent Winter Gardens seen from the corner of Coronation Walk and the Promenade, 1880. The gardens covered an area of 9 acres. Within the complex were conservatories, promenade walkways, an auditorium for 2,000 people, an aquarium and roller skating rink. To the left is the public vault of the Royal Hotel. Today it is the Royal Clifton Hotel.

The south end of the then boating lake, later Marine Lake, with one of the towers of the cableway which crossed the lake, 1890s. A passenger-carrying gondola is visible on the cable, centre skyline. Crowds throng what was at this time a fairground.

Early site preparations for the North Marine Lake, early 1890s. Work began on 19 January 1891 and was hampered by some unusually high tides. This may well show one such tide coming into the excavated area of the proposed lake from the right. Alternatively it could be at the end of the excavations in the early part of 1892, for it was opened on 20 June by the mayor of Southport.

The onlookers certainly seem to be enthralled by the spectacle of the incoming sea. And what about the three-masted ship? Was it moored, or yet another wreck on the beach?

The North Marine Lake and the Children's Beach, *c.* 1900. A sand beach had been formed during construction, into the lake itself. It was used as a paddling pool for many years.

More paddlers at the Marine Lake, early 1900s. There still seems to be a lack of swimming costumes.

The south end of the former boating lake looking across to the Kings Gardens on the Promenade, 1920s. Compare this much-altered area with the bottom picture on page 26. Here the fairground has been moved.

Looking north along the Promenade and Kings Gardens from the corner of the Esplanade. As yet the Floral Hall does not appear to have been built. The original sea wall followed the line of the wide footpath.

The first fairground on Southport's seafront, featuring helter-skelter, water chute and captive flying machines. This postcard was sent from Southport to Oxford on 13 July 1910. The stamp cost a ha'penny.

The imposing entrance to the fairground, 1926. Resited away from the Promenade in the period 1910 to 1920, it stands by the Esplanade. It was set out on a grander scale than its predecessor and covered a larger area.

Looking south-west across Kings Gardens and the end of the boating lake to the much larger amusement park in the distance with its entrance and flying machines. The buses in the foreground are, in front, a charabanc belonging to Abrams Safety Coaches, and, behind, an early Ribble Motors bus.

Taken from almost the same vantage point as the picture above, this view dates from about 1950, some twenty-five years on. There have been some changes to the amusement park it seems, when one compares the pictures. The open-top bus was used for rides along the sands and seafront.

A panoramic view, looking from the end of Neville Street southwards along the Promenade, *c.* 1958. In the immediate foreground is the statue of Queen Victoria by Sir George Frampton, which stood originally outside the Atkinson Art Gallery in Lord Street, where it was unveiled in 1904. It was resited at the request of the sculptor. Located upper centre, on the curve of the 'Prom' to the Esplanade, is the back of the Garrick Theatre, beyond that Rotten Row with the site of the annual flower show, Victoria Park, visible top centre. To the right of the Promenade are the Kings Gardens with their attractive flower beds. The boating lake and bowling greens also feature. Beyond the boating lake, in the distance, a railway footbridge spans the former Cheshire Lines Railway, whose tracks ran across the photograph to the extreme left, where, fronting on to Lord Street, the railway station stood.

The enlarged day nursery for visitors' children on Marine Parade, close to the pier, in the 1920s. Started by Mayoress Mary Willets in about 1908, the scheme had proved extremely popular.

Across the road from the day nursery was Peter Pan's Pool and Playground, an area specifically designated for use by young children. It adjoined the Children's Beach. The site, renamed Happiland, is still in use today.

The North Marine Lake looking over to the Promenade in the middle of this century. The Children's Beach is to the left.

Smiling passengers 'back in time for tea', having enjoyed a boat trip around the Marine Lake during the 1950s.

Situated between Promenade and Marine Lake are the Floral Hall Gardens, seen here with most of the deck chairs taken, their occupants listening to a concert by the Ed Harper band, *c.* 1965. Just visible in the centre of the horizon and across the River Ribble estuary is Blackpool Tower. Note the parked 'bubble car'. How many still survive into the 1990s?

The Floral Hall Gardens café packed with customers, mid-1950s.

The model boating lake in Princes Park, near the open-air bathing lake, 1950s. These snapshots will bring back many happy memories for those of us who were regular visitors here, clad in short trousers to sail our mostly modest yachts. And we took it very seriously, too.

The model boating lake again, this time looking the opposite way, towards Pleasureland. The two children standing by the edge are definite scene-stealers even amid all the activity.

Aerial view of the south end of the Marine Drive which runs diagonally across, from bottom left to almost top right. In the immediate foreground is the pier. In the bottom left-hand corner is the roundabout, around which one drove from Marine Parade, to get on to the sands and park. This is the early 1960s, and as yet the Marine Drive alongside the beach had not been built; today it runs north from the roundabout at the bottom left. From the number of cars on the beach it must have been a nice day, and a scene which is repeated every weekend in the season. Dominating the scene, though, is the Sea Bathing Lake, its distinct oval shape (on the seaward side of Princes Park) sadly gone now, demolished within the last two years. The salt may have got into your eyes, but it was a good place to go. Perhaps today's youngsters are not as tough, or perhaps they have more sense than their parents had, for it was never really warm in the water, was it? Pity it couldn't have been covered with a dome, though. . . .

Pleasureland is to the right of centre, and beyond, just visible, are the sandhills at Ainsdale. The curving route of the Cheshire Lines Railway can also be made out, just above Pleasureland. Closed in the early 1950s, its trains used to run to the terminus station in Lord Street.

Memories of how it used to be, inside the Sea Bathing Lake on a hot summer's day, 1960s. Sheltered from the wind, it was a good place for sunbathing too. The opening ceremony for the new bathing lake, which was built on the site of an earlier open air pool, was performed by Lord Derby in 1928. The building costs were £70,000. The oval pool was 110 yards long and held over one and a half million gallons of seawater supplied by pumps positioned at the sea end of the pier. In the mid-1960s, a new filtration system was installed at a cost of £35,000. The curved steps in the centre of the picture used to be the venue for the many bathing beauty and 'English Rose' competitions.

Aerial view of Southport town and foreshore, mid-1960s. The complete layout of the Promenade and foreshore area is clearly illustrated, their appearance recently changed owing to the demolition of the bathing lake and the Colonnade, both in Princes Park.

Here, the tree-lined Lord Street runs from left to right, and Chapel Street railway station roof is visible at the centre, bottom edge. To the right of the station, London Street runs into Nevill Street, then on to the Promenade, where Queen Victoria's statue watches over the foreshore area. In the centre is the original boating lake dating from 1887, which in 1895 was joined to the 'new' northern lake which had been built on the other (north) side of the pier. Above the boating lake is Princes Park, approached by a walkway with bridge crossing over the middle of the lake. Within the park, near the entrance is the Colonnade, a curved open-air building, in which many concert parties and bands entertained the visitor. Beyond lies the Sea Bathing Lake. Pleasureland is to the left, and the Peter Pan play area to the right. All is laid out in a pleasing manner.

Looking northwards along the foreshore area. Taken from a vantage point to the left of that used on the facing page, many of the same features can be seen here too. The symmetry of the bridge in the lake and the approach to the bathing lake are shown to particular advantage. The curving line of the Promenade is to the right-hand side, following the exact line of the first sea wall constructed in the 1850s. At that time the sea covered the whole of the rest of the area left of the Promenade; reclamation here has been going on since the 1880s. The width of the North Marine Lake was further increased in the early 1960s, the original, seaward side of the lake being detectable from the straight edges of the two islands created during the works. With this extension, a new coastal road was built, over a mile long, which can be seen disappearing into the distance. With the building of this new road, a further 90 acres of land was reclaimed from the sea.

Looking across the boating lake, the bridge in the middle, with the Colonnade and Sea Bathing Lake in the distance, 1950s.

Looking south to the Floral Hall in the centre and the Marine Lake, with its flotilla of yachts being prepared for an afternoon's sailing, mid-1960s. This photograph was taken from the corner of Seabank Road and the Promenade.

Section Three

THAT'S ENTERTAINMENT

Birtwistle's Buildings . .
Corporation St , Southport.
1870
1905
PROGRAMME
OF
THE EMPLOYES OF
WM. ASHTON & SONS LTD.
First
Annual...
Social Evening and Dance
Tuesday,
November 21st,
1905.
8 TO 2.
COMMENCE
8 P.M.
PROMPT.
M.C.'s :
Messrs. Gillibrand & Redfern.

Programme card for Messrs William Ashton & Sons Limited's social evening, 21 November 1905. Inside the card is a list of the dances. To round off all this 'frantic excitement', 'gramophone records will be played by Mr Hy Sancto'.

‘Standing room only’ at this band concert held in the Municipal Gardens on Lord Street in the early 1900s. Always a popular venue from its earliest days, here, for a small fee, you could sit and listen to local and visiting bands.

The interior of the former Palais de Danse, Lord Street. Opened in 1925, it was reputed to have had the largest parquet floor then in existence, costing £3,000 to install. Billy Cotton’s Band played here for a while. Sadly, after only a few years it was converted to the Trocadero Cinema. A branch of Woolworths now stands on the site; the Lord Street entrance is where the ‘Palais’ used to be.

The Picturedrome near the Prince of Wales Hotel, Lord Street. A purpose-built cinema, it was opened in 1910. The film showing is *The World in Motion*, with matinees each afternoon and evening performances at 7 and 9 p.m. The seat prices are 1*s*, 6*d* and 3*d*. Note the side entrance to the lowest priced seats.

The imposing frontage of another Southport cinema, the Picture Palace, *c.* 1920. Its prices were as at the Picturedrome, but it also had boxes, at 10*s* and 6*d*. The films showing are *Picturesque Devonshire* and *Janet's Flirtation*.

Hilda O'Byrne (née Gillibrand) was born in Nelson Street, Southport, in 1899. Pictured here in her twenties, now married to Frank Napier O'Byrne, she became part of the variety duo 'Napier and Joan'. (She is also seen aged three, with her mother, on page 103.)

Frank Napier O'Byrne, an American, married Hilda Gillibrand. A vaudeville artist who played worldwide, he also appeared in a Royal Command Performance for King George V. During the 1920s and '30s he became a cinema manager at Southport's Palladium.

The Municipal Gardens with their new bandstand, May 1924. The band are about to commence their first concert of the season. The larger improved seating area complemented the classical design of the bandstand.

The bandstand with the Southport Corporation Military Band, their wonderful array of instruments proudly displayed, mid-1930s.

Southport Opera House, Lord Street, situated next to the Cheshire Lines railway station with its clock tower, *c.* 1920. Built in 1891 as part of the Winter Gardens complex, it had seating for 2,000. The original building was destroyed by fire in 1929 but a new theatre arose from the ashes. . . .

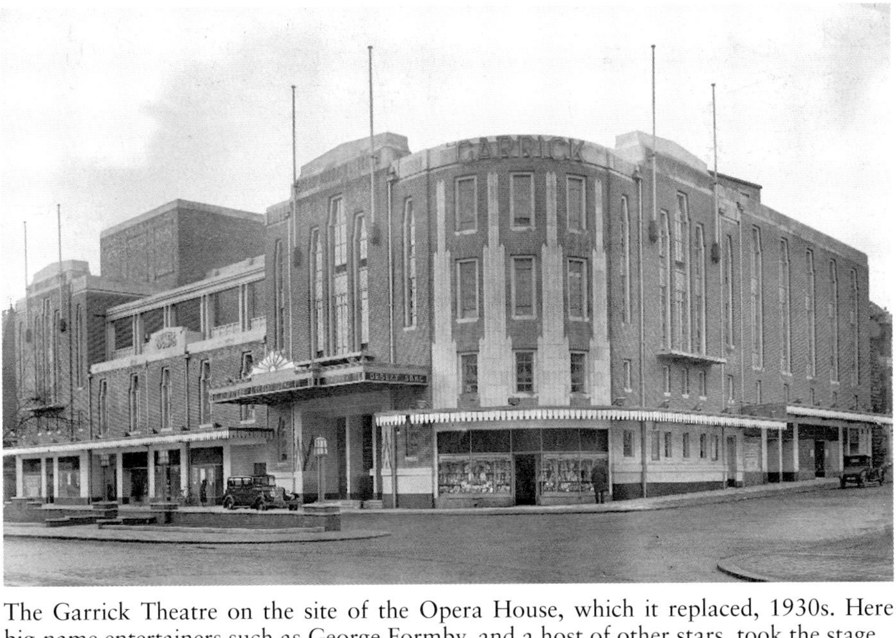

The Garrick Theatre on the site of the Opera House, which it replaced, 1930s. Here big-name entertainers such as George Formby, and a host of other stars, took the stage.

The Floral Hall Gardens looking south to the Promenade and Kings Gardens. A large audience is enjoying a concert, probably during the 1930s. Today large numbers also enjoy the garden concerts, although modern dress seems to be considerably more casual, but little else has changed. Note the Victoria Baths to the left of the bandstand, with Queen Victoria's statue at the end of Nevill Street visible above it. The baths' façade, as we know it today, was a result of the extensions and general improvements carried out in 1871, the original baths having been constructed in 1839.

Inside the Floral Hall during a band concert, January 1939. The faces in the audience look rather serious. Is it because of the political situation in Europe. Or perhaps the café had run out of tea?

The Ed Harper band in 1959. Only their leader, standing close to the BBC microphone, is smiling. Band concerts were often broadcast to the nation from the Floral Hall.

The Colonnade, another foreshore building now just a memory, with a concert under way in the 1950s. This horseshoe-shaped building had a stage on which concert parties and small bands played to audiences seated on deck chairs. Towards the end of its life, the auditorium was converted into a roller skating rink.

The open-air theatre at the end of the pier, mid-1950s. It almost looks like the deck of a ship because the horizon is the sea. Actually the water is the River Ribble estuary, with a very faint Blackpool Tower in the distance.

The bandstand in the Floral Hall Gardens, moved to the side by the early 1950s. The installation of a tannoy system, its numerous loudspeakers fitted to the roof of the bandstand, ensured that there were no problems hearing the music.

Listening to the band in the Municipal Gardens, 1950s. If you got there early enough, you might get a bit of colour sitting in the sun, away from the shade of the trees.

Above, the Floral Hall Gardens in the 1950s. Below, the gardens in the mid-1960s. The audience did not come only to hear the band; as the gardens are so sheltered, it is also a good spot for sunbathing. Surprisingly large numbers of the men are wearing jackets, some even sport waistcoats. But the ladies at least are getting their legs sunburnt.

The Municipal Gardens, Lord Street, with the wonderful classically inspired bandstand. During the improvements to the gardens in the 1920s, a new stand was built to replace the cast-iron stand, and a tiled and patterned seating area was created. Now a fountain stands on the site and the bandstand has gone. Many feel the change makes for a less attractive view, but it's a matter of opinion.

The young lady morris dancers are from the group run by Mrs Hull from Birkdale. The names of only two participants have come to light: a Miss Page and a Miss Brenda Stead. Apologies to the other troupe members not named; at least the picture should evoke some pleasant memories.

Southport Theatre, forming a sort of extension to the Floral Hall which it adjoins, mid-1970s. Built in the early 1970s, it took over the role of theatre, lost to Southport with the closure of the Garrick. A regular venue for famous international celebrities and stars, it is often on the tour itinerary for top recording artists. The first to appear, following the gala opening of the complex in May 1973, was the one and only Marlene Dietrich. Here the girls are queueing for a concert featuring their idols, the Bay City Rollers – hence the flares and tartans. Many of the fans here are probably mothers now; I wonder if the photograph will be shown to their children, to illustrate how 'mum' was dressing in the swinging '70s.

Section Four

MAINLY LORD STREET

A painting of Lord Street and its shops, 1858. The developing Southport of the 1830s and '40s saw the beginning of the street as we know it today, but it was only in the 1880s and '90s that the layout of the street was properly planned.

Looking across to the 'shopping side' of the street. The trams and horses would seem to give this scene a pre-1914 date.

Members of Southport Car Club posing outside the Scarisbrick Hotel, before a run, *c.* 1905. Considering the year, when cars had not been around too long, the club must have been one of the earliest to be formed in the then county of Lancashire.

A postcard view of the old bandstand with nearby ornamental pond, December 1905. This area was altered in the 1920s, to create a tiled area, for additional seating. Compare this with the view on page 55 featuring the morris dancers.

Number 8 tram, on the circle route, passing along Lord Street. Electric trams began working in Southport in 1900, mainly replacing the horse-drawn trams which had started up in 1873. The trams served the town until 1934. Now that tram transport is once again in favour, perhaps the 'boulevard' of Lord Street will see them again.

The imposing dimensions of Lord Street with shops to the left and the wide ribbon of gardens to the right, *c.* 1930. Behind the latter were many private houses in the early years which later became shops and hotels.

The street looking to the north, some of the shops with canopies over the footpath, including one of the oldest in Lord Street, Boothroyds, established in 1825. The photograph probably dates from the mid-1930s.

The Municipal Gardens café, *c.* 1920. Apart from the men's straw hats, an astonishing seven other types of headgear are being worn. Strange, but there's hardly a lady in sight. (See also the front cover.)

The Municipal Gardens café, *c.* 1934. It looks as busy as ever and the waiter service is still an essential part of this seemingly very social meeting place.

The Cenotaph, London Square, Lord Street, early 1930s. The names of all Southport's citizens who lost their lives in the past wars are recorded in two pavilions, located to each side of the Cenotaph.

The Cenotaph, probably late 1930s. Note that the tram tracks have gone.

It was still possible to park in Lord Street in the 1950s, and, it seems, possible to get over the road without zebra crossings!

Aside from the double-decker bus, this view of Lord Street, wide and tree-lined, gives the continental air so often ascribed to the thoroughfare. The photograph probably dates from the late 1950s.

The junction of Eastbank Street with Lord Street with a policeman on point duty at the corner, early 1950s. To the right is the imposing Atkinson Art Gallery building, opened in 1878. Next to this is the Town Hall, housed in what was once a private house dating from the early 1850s.

Eastbank Street, early 1950s. From the left, the shops in this view are Irwins, Wildings, Stead & Simpson, Morris, and Sharples.

The wide footpath in front of the shops on Lord Street. The canopies, constructed from decorated cast iron, provide cover to browse in the shop windows even on days of inclement weather.

Looking across Lord Street from London Square and the Cenotaph to some of the street's most interesting architectural features. The building to the right is the National Provincial, next door is Martins Bank (formerly the Bank of Liverpool), then Barclays and the 'Elizabethan' gables of the Albany Building. Situated just behind the trees is the former Preston Bank, built in the style of Roman classical architecture.

Shops and shoppers, 1952. Note that the original flat canopies have been replaced with the curved type.

More shoppers, probably late 1940s. The canopy support and decorated wooden edging are a little reminiscent of the type still seen in some railway stations.

Speaking of railway canopies . . . Chapel Street railway station, terminus of the former Lancashire and Yorkshire Railway in Southport. This rail link was the first to Manchester, via Wigan, and was opened, single line only, in 1855, a distance of 17 miles from Wigan. The company had opened an electric line from Liverpool in 1902.

An advertisement for Southport displayed at London's Euston station in 1929. It was an eye-catching 20 feet long by 6 feet high. And just look at those ticket prices! Third class, tourist, 49*s* and 6*d*, and period excursion, 36*s* and 6*d*. Today, the cheapest period fare from Southport to London is £25.

Southport Chapel Street station with the immaculate former LMS 'Jubilee' class steam locomotive 45717 *Dauntless*, 13 April 1955. The occasion was the visit of Her Majesty the Queen, although it is not certain if *Dauntless* was pulling the royal train or was on other duties.

From trains to trams . . . Chapel Street, 18 July 1900. On that day Southport's horse-drawn trams were first powered by electricity. Here two specially decorated trams are carrying local officials. A large crowd turned up to witness the event, including many photographers to record the scene for posterity. Note the man with box camera left of centre.

Some of the staff employed by the Electric Tramway Company, with the drivers/conductors in very smart uniforms, before the First World War. The system soon proved to be a popular method of transportation, and several picture postcards of the early trams were soon issued and bought by visitors to be sent home.

The staff of the Cheshire Lines Railway station on Lord Street in 1927. The service brought not only LMS railway trains but those from the LNE as well, and was a busy place in the season. The station closed in 1952, later to become a bus station.

The approach to the station at Lord Street, under the road bridge between the Promenade and Rotten Row, *c.* 1950. The clock tower, fronting the station, stands beyond the bridge and platforms.

The Cheshire Lines station, Lord Street, and the layout of the platforms at the terminus, late 1940s. The way out into the street was through the booking hall, beyond the wall at the end of the platform.

The lively scene inside the former Sea Bathing Lake in the 1930s, captured on a poster by the artist Fortunino Matania. Along with other old railway memorabilia, ranging from engine name and number plates to crockery and old tickets, railway posters are becoming very collectable. We all remember them, some perhaps for a special reason, such as a wonderful holiday, or perhaps as illustrating somewhere we always wanted to get to, and never did. The posters depicted places which always looked attractive and inviting. They did their job, in fact; that seaside view on the hoarding caught your eye and stuck in your mind. Some of the artists commissioned to produce the posters created more than just an advertisement; they painted scenes with much detail and animation. One such painter was Fortunino Matania RI, whose work is featured on this poster for Cheshire Lines Railway, one of several he produced for Southport.

The information display stand for Southport at the Home Life Exhibition at London's Alexandra Palace, October 1929. 'Sunny Southport, the all seasons holiday resort on the Lancashire Coast', the main notice proclaims, 'for residence, health and pleasure.' Some of the smaller notices advertise the Flower Show for 1929, or a week-end in Southport, 35*s* 6*d* return from Euston. To the right-hand side of the stand, a notice advertises a set of lantern slides of Southport on an illuminated board. Among the town's attractions, it was 'England's Garden City' with a 'Water supply, No Purer in Nature . . . Remarkably Pure Air, Fog Almost Unknown . . . Rates 8/8 in the Pound . . . Population 78,000'.

Section Five

HORSES & HORSE POWER

A one horse power 'leafing' cart, belonging to Southport Corporation Health Committee on a collection round, c. 1890. Notice the hinged door on the side of the cart and the brush to sweep up the fallen leaves.

Loading up the bread delivery van at Birkdale, where a 'farm school' was located in the early years of the twentieth century. As with many establishments at that time, it was always short of money so, to supplement funds, bread was baked and sold then deliveries made to shops in the area.

Sam Banner's wine and spirits shop, probably located on the corner of Shakespeare Street and Portland Street, *c.* 1911. Here also a horse and cart were used to effect deliveries of 'wines, spirits, ales and stouts'.

A two-horse tram outside the Botanical Gardens, *c.* 1885. Introduced in 1873, Southport's two-horse trams worked between Churchtown and Birkdale, travelling through Lord Street en route. They were actually in operation until 1902, although electric trams were introduced in 1900.

Pioneer steam car, made in Surrey, with its owners Mr and Mrs Saville Paris and driver outside their Walmer Road house, *c.* 1906. Steam-powered cars were used between the horse-drawn carriage period and the advent of the petrol-driven vehicle.

The business premises of Joseph and Thomas Hampson, who started up their motor engineering works in Southport in 1898. Their early cars were a great success, and were called Vulcan. The enterprise grew quickly, necessitating a move to new premises in Crossens in 1906.

A very early Vulcan car, dating from about 1903, being scrutinized by the locals. They are probably wondering whether it will ever catch on. . . .

The two Hampson brothers, both nearest to camera, founders of Vulcan Motors, sitting in one of the vehicles produced at their Crossens factory. The radiator mascot of the Vulcan was a blacksmith standing by an anvil.

Some of the Vulcan manufacturing staff in front of their offices, a works which employed 700 in its heyday. It ceased car production in 1928. Before the move to the new Crossens premises, the company had a capital of some £10,000; its full name was Vulcan Motor Manufacturing and Engine Company. Southport's first bus was built by the company in 1924.

The Promenade with the Victoria Baths to the right. Judging by the fashions being worn, and the design of the car, this view dates from about 1905.

A vehicle forgotten and submerged by the waves in the first decade of the twentieth century. Any metal detectors working the beach would get a bit of a surprise if they found a car like this today!

A 'chara trip' out of Southport in the early 1920s. Such trips usually went inland. Sometimes 'mystery trips' from the seaside might take you back to your home town!

A charabanc convoy, fronted by a huge Leyland with two Daimlers behind, parked outside the Coliseum, *c.* 1925. They are about to set off for Aintree to watch the Grand National.

An open-topped vehicle, possibly one of the first police cars to have been used in Southport, in about the late 1920s.

Tram Number 36, a 'Toast-rack'. Southport's tram system, electrified from 1900, was used until New Year's Eve 1934, when the system was dismantled. Between 1914 and 1931 the 'Toast-rack' trams were in service during the summer months.

Looking north along Lord Street, *c.* 1930. The bus on the right is one of the locally built Vulcans and is en route to Guildford Road via Liverpool Road.

An interesting group of cars, parked on the Promenade, near Kings Gardens, taking part in a 'Motoring Weekend' in 1954.

Looking towards the back of the Floral Hall from the Marine Parade Bridge, with the Marine Lake to the left, late 1950s. The car park has an interesting selection of vehicles, including many of the popular Bedford Dormobiles.

A battery operated refuse truck in Albert Road, *c.* 1960. The three-man team of council workers includes Harry Whiteside (left) and Peter Tinsley (right).

Lord Street, featuring Austins, Humbers, Consuls and Anglias, early 1960s. By the beginning of the nineteenth century Lord Street was becoming established as the centre of the growing township. A new canal route from Manchester to Scarisbrick, some 15 miles away, was operating by 1820; this was in addition to the extant passenger route on the canal from Liverpool, opened in 1777. Coaches carried visitors from Scarisbrick into Southport at this time. The year 1821 was very significant for the town, as many people came to live here. In 1822 the growing town had three inns, three chapels, a drapers, a tailors, a druggists and some twenty grocer's shops, all either in or close to Lords Street, as it was then called.

By 1840 the west side of the street mainly comprised shops. But on the other side of the street were private houses with long gardens. The latter later formed the long, green ribbon of trees and flower beds for which the street is famous – the Municipal Gardens, today so much enjoyed by the visitors and townsfolk of Southport.

Collective horse power in a display of new Southport Corporation 'spreader' vehicles in their depot, near to the former St Lukes railway station, seen here behind the vehicles. The photograph dates from the mid-1950s.

A Southport council 'gully wagon' sucking the drains or 'gullies' clear of blockages. Here a Dennis vehicle from the 1950s performs the job with Nick McCoombe holding the suction pipe.

Emptying dustbins in Shakespeare Street, early 1960s. Now a thing of the past, note the man's sack-cloth 'cape'. On the right is the Ensign cycle shop.

Resurfacing in Guildford Road using a 'cold planer', 1950s. The actual planing operation is being done by the vehicle to the right. The surface removed is being fed into the rear of the Bedford truck to the left.

Workmen repairing the road surface for the increasing number of vehicles in the late 1950s. Above, a Latil tractor towing 'sledges' which are filling hollows in the surface of the road. Below, laying hot bitumen to the surface of Scarisbrick New Road in 1957. Both activities were always good for 'spectating', but not quite as good as the old tar and cobbles work that was done!

Beach parking close to the Sea Bathing Lake and Pleasureland, mid-1960s. Children were never satisfied with being on the beach if their parents parked here; the slides and roundabouts of the Pleasureland complex were a greater attraction.

Looking south along the beach from the pier, with the Sea Bathing Lake to the left and the Pleasureland 'Cyclone' in the distance. And what a wealth of collectable motor cars, among them Ford Consuls, Vauxhall Crestas and Standard Pennants.

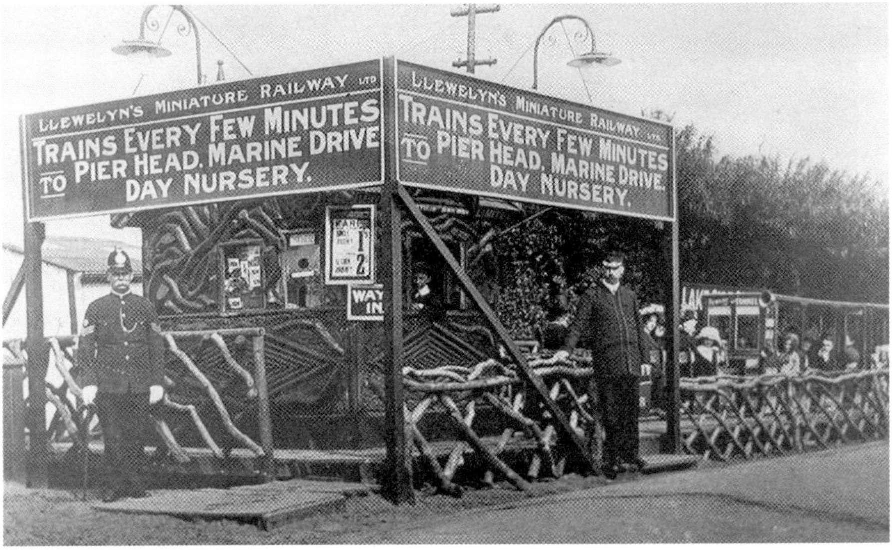

The south end of the line of the half-mile long Lakeside Miniature Railway with the owner, Mr Llewelyn, standing to the right below the sign, 1911.

The Lakeside Miniature Railway's 15-in gauge steam locomotive *King George V* with Mr Llewelyn to the right, 1912.

Nellie, one of the steam locomotive engines designed by Emett (the cartoonist) and built by Harry Barlow at his Southport workshop, being photographed before going to London in early 1951 to take part in the Festival of Britain, held at Battersea Park that year.

Nellie with tender, and the logo 'Far Tottering and Oyster Creek Railway'. After the Festival of Britain the engine was rebuilt at Battersea and continued in use there, eventually returning to Southport in 1954, and becoming the *Princess Anne*. Of the other two engines, the *Wild Goose* returned to Southport to be rebuilt as the *Prince Charles*.

The rebuilt *Prince Charles* engine on the Lakeside Miniature Railway, emerging from below the pier to run down to the station extension line. The railway has five locomotives, one of these being a modern reconstruction of the 1909 steam locomotive *Red Dragon*.

A new locomotive, the *Duke of Edinburgh*, at its official naming ceremony in 1948. Various local dignitaries were in attendance together with the BBC, whose interviewer can be seen here in the cab seat of the new engine.

Section Six

THE SPORTING LIFE

'Sandhurst Cricket Club, First Year of League.' The cricket team and officials display their cup, c. *1920.*

Southport's Blowick Juniors Football Club in 1936. Left to right, back row: M. Hulme, S. Leach, D. Hargreaves, K. Smith, L. Watkins, O. Blundell, E. Jones, W. Little. Front row: C. Ball, J. Eccles, R. Gibson, N. France, J. Little, W. Armitage.

The bowling green in Kings Gardens, adjoining the Esplanade, 1950s.

The Marine Lake, mid-1950s. Yachting, wind surfing and water skiing are among the popular sports on offer. The Lancashire Yacht Club and the Southport Sailing Club both have their headquarters here.

Norwood Road Junior School football team, 1971. The only two players identified are Paul Longworth (back row, third from right) and Gary Marriot (front row, second from right). The school was demolished during the 1980s.

A 'sprint trial' organized by Southport Motor Club, early 1900s. These were held on the Promenade where stands were built for spectators. The cars were timed over a distance, from a standing start, but there were no races. This sprint seems to be under way on the wide footpath. Note the early photographers at the bottom left.

Southport and Ainsdale Beach was used for motor racing in the 1920s. Although the majority of drivers were men, a few ladies did compete. May Cunliffe, whose father was also a driver here, seated in her car, sometime during 1928.

Jack Field, a Southport garage owner, initially a spectator at beach racing in the early 1920s, began racing himself in 1928, having purchased a two-litre Bugatti. Jack raced at Southport, Phoenix Park, and at the world-famous Brooklands circuit in 1930.

A display of some of the many trophies won by the Field 'stable' along with the car, called 'Hell's Angel'. Officially it was a 'special', originally purchased from Henry Seagrave, with a spare engine from Malcolm Campbell. This car was also a regular competitor at the Brooklands circuit.

Jack Field in his Bugatti type 43, 1929. He was a regular performer in the beach races.

Driven at speed on Southport Beach, the 2.3 litre Bugatti formerly owned by Malcolm Campbell. This car often exceeded 100 m.p.h. on the Brooklands track. Here in Southport, during 1932 and 1933, it won forty-four races, and gained a second in the Southport 100 Mile race.

The 'Silver Bullet' on Birkdale Beach, and mechanic Carlo Querico (with beret) carrying out adjustments before a run, *c.* 1935. The two wheels to the right are spares, the wheel in the centre is the car's right front.

The Sunbeam 'Silver Bullet' was driven by Kaye Don at Daytona Beach, USA in 1930, in an attempt to break Malcolm Campbell's record speed of 217 m.p.h. This, and subsequent attempts with 'Silver Bullet', were unsuccessful. The car was brought back to England, where it was eventually purchased by Southport's Jack Field. On arrival in Southport in 1934 the car was paraded through the streets where large crowds turned out to see this spectacular machine which had featured so prominently in recent newspapers and on radio. It was quite a car . . . 31 ft long, weighing 3 tons, with two 12-cylinder engines, one behind the other, capable of generating 4,000 horse power.

Two mechanics who had worked on the car in America were Charles Cooper and Carlo Querico, for it was prone to supercharger and cooling system problems, ice having to be used to keep the engine cool. The car had to be started using compressed air. If it didn't start first time, all twenty-four plugs had to be cleaned.

Despite many attempts to run the car at high speed, problems arose regularly, which led to the car being sold to another enthusiast, Fred Dixon.

Another former Malcolm Campbell car which was at Southport for some time was the Sunbeam V12. With a 350 horse power capacity it was capable of speeds in excess of 150 m.p.h. When purchased by Jack Field in 1936, it was owned by Ralph Aspden, and it was the intention of Field to beat the 'Southport Flying Mile' record.

Despite several attempts to attain the new record, and with a great deal of spectator interest, the car did not reach the anticipated speed. Eventually, unable to improve its performance, Jack Field sold the car to an up-and-coming bandleader, Bill Cotton, who had driven Bugattis on several occasions on Southport Beach. Bill's mechanics were able to carry out some adjustments which did improve the car's performance. Again it was entered for the Southport 100 Mile race, this time achieving a speed of 121 m.p.h., and winning for its owner the Southport 100 Gold Badge. The car has been preserved and can be seen at Beaulieu Motor Museum.

The Dunlop Professional Tournament, with Henry Cotton the star attraction on the eighteenth hole, apparently lining up a putt, 1933.

The Dunlop Tournament, 1946. The competition is over, and the winner, Max Faulkner, is being presented with a cheque for £365 by Mayor and Alderman S.E. Charlton.

One of the golfing calendar's most important international competitions, the Ryder Cup tournament between Great Britain and the USA, held at the Southport and Ainsdale Golf Club in 1933. The club joint committee for the event is seen here. The chairman, Mr T.H. Thomas, is seated in the centre of the front row; the secretary, Mr G.N. Openshaw, is on the extreme right.

The British Ryder Cup team players, 1933. Back row, left to right: A. Perry, A. Daily, A.G. Havers, C.A. Whitcombe, S. Easterbrook, Capt. Stark (trainer). Front row: A.J. Lacey, A.H. Padgham, W.H. Davies, J.H. Taylor (non-playing captain), Abe Mitchell, P. Allis.

Crowds hurrying from the seventh to the eighth hole to gain the best vantage point during the Ryder Cup match of 1933. On the first day, Monday 26 June, a crowd of some seven thousand attended. The stewards controlled them with long bamboo poles to which red flags were attached, earning themselves the nickname of 'the Ainsdale Lancers'. At the end of that day, the Great Britain team were in the lead by 2½ points to 1½. On Tuesday, the second day of play, the crowd figure was estimated to have increased to twenty thousand, the 'Ainsdale Lancers' being hard pressed to control the large numbers. The matches played this second day comprised eight 'very exciting' singles. At the end of this day, the British team again finished ahead. Great Britain won the cup with a total of 6½ points to the US team's 5½.

On this second day, HRH the Prince of Wales attended, having been driven over from Liverpool, to be greeted by flag-waving, cheering children. After watching the closing stages of the match, he presented the Ryder Cup to the non-playing captain of the Great Britain team, Mr J.H. Taylor. Both the British and American team members were presented with medals by the Prince of Wales, after which he returned to Liverpool. The evening came to an end with a celebration dinner for players, officials and local dignitaries, held, appropriately, in the Prince of Wales Hotel.

Horton Smith (GB), to the right, putting on the second hole with Charles Whitcombe (USA), centre, watching the putt during their match for the Ryder Cup in 1933.

The end of the Ryder Cup match, 1933. Here HRH the Prince of Wales presents the cup to the Great Britain Captain J.H. Taylor on the clubhouse veranda of the Southport and Ainsdale Golf Club, Tuesday 27 June 1933. Both countries had now won the cup on two occasions in the series.

Section Eight

PEOPLE & EVENTS

Mrs Elizabeth Ann Gillibrand (née Walmsley), with daughter Hilda aged three, 1902. They lived in Nelson Street, Southport. (A grown up Hilda is pictured on page 46.)

The ill-fated lifeboat *Eliza Fearnley* on the beach. On 10 December 1886, she overturned during the stormy night while attempting to rescue the crew of the German barque *Mexico*. She was lost with all her hands except two. The lifeboat from St Annes, across the Ribble estuary, also lost her full crew, a total of twenty-seven men perishing. The incident occasioned the greatest loss of life in the lifeboat service in the country.

The *Mexico*, washed ashore the day after the storm, is seen here on the beach, the crew having been got off safely by a lifeboat from Lytham. Shortly afterwards the barque was made watertight and towed to a mooring off Lytham, and later refitted to put to sea again.

The lifeboat *Mary Anna*, which followed the *Eliza Fearnley*, being towed through Eastbank Street, probably on a Lifeboat Day during the 1890s. The boat was commissioned in 1886, and was followed by three others: the *Edith and Annie* in 1888, the *Three Brothers* in 1902 (demonstrated only), and the last 'true' lifeboat, the *John Harling* in 1904.

An undated postcard showing Southport lifeboatmen at the turn of the century. Henry Robinson (eighth from left), was one of the two survivors of the *Mexico* tragedy of 1886. Fourteen Southport lifeboatmen lost their lives that fateful night. A monument to their memory stands on the promenade by Kings Gardens.

Benjamin Gillibrand of Southport (b. 1863), photographed here in 1900. Benjamin worked for William Ashton and Sons, publishers of the *Southport Journal*, for thirty years, becoming managing editor. He retired in 1927.

A 'thrilling' race being run by five ladies on the Athletics Ground, *c.* 1905. No shorts and T-shirts here, they had to cope with long dresses and hats into the bargain. The event is an egg and spoon race.

A postcard of C. Grahame-White, a famous aviator of the time, 23 June 1911. He is seen here on the occasion of Southport's 'Flying Circus' which took place then at Blowick, a suburb of the town. In later years air races were held in Southport.

A civic affair, precise circumstances unknown, with army officers and clergy. What was going on? Why were they all assembled? The year may be 1914 or 1915 when the mayor shown was Mr J.E. Willett CBE, DL, JP. But he had other periods in office as well!

The Mayor Mr E. Hadfield OBE holding a prize marrow at the Southport Flower Show, 1925. The smiling group was a rare sight on most 1920s photographs. I wonder what the mayor was saying.

The official opening of the Sea Bathing Lake in Princes Park, 1928. Lord Derby, centre, is about to cut the ceremonial 'opening' ribbon following the playing of the National Anthem.

Visitors to the Southport Flower Show admiring the rock garden displays, 1948. This was the second postwar show, for the event had been suspended during the war years.

The wedding of Florence May Rimmer (née Ibbotson), who was 'in service' at Birkdale, and Charles Rimmer, who was 'in building', at Mornington Road church, Southport, 17 October 1931.

Chapel Street station platform with a group of boys from Christ Church School about to board their train for an educational trip, 1937. The headmaster, Mr Thompson, is in the back row, fourth from the right; he doesn't appear to be looking forward to the trip. . . .

An Orangemen's Parade passing along one of Southport's streets, 1951. It seems to have attracted quite a number of spectators.

Ten young ladies, forming themselves into a letter 'W', taking part in the Wolsey Bathing Parade held in the Sea Bathing Lake on 24 August 1929. The lake had been opened the previous year.

A bathing beauty competition in 1944 being held to lift morale during the war years.

Some of the entrants to an 'English Rose' competition during the late 1940s or early '50s. These competitions were held in heats which started in midsummer, with the final selection of a winner taking place in September. The girls had to get through a two-stage selection, first dressed in day clothes and then in bathing costumes.

Southport's annual 'English Rose' competition, 1950. But the usual venue, the Sea Bathing Lake, seems to have been avoided, for this view is of the Municipal Gardens in Lord Street. From about this time it was customary to get one of the celebrities who were appearing in the theatres of the town to present the prizes, at that time £600 to the winner. Here film star Dennis Price is doing the honours.

Miss Pat Kershaw, winner of the 1951 'English Rose' competition. Miss Kershaw was presented with her cheque by Norman Evans, star of theatre and radio.

A wonderfully balanced pose, probably arranged by the geometry master, of Form 5, Birkdale Secondary Modern School, 1952. Back row, left to right: John Asworth, Barry Everett, Tony Hindley. Centre row: Gladys Mullard, Barbara Rimmer, Muriel Makinson, Brenda Wignall, Joyce Prescott, Betty Nickson, Judith Bedford. Front row: Valerie Coley, Rosemary Blanchard, Mr Manning (Deputy Head), Mr Holroyd (Headmaster), Mr Russell (Form 5 Tutor), Vera Rimmer, Freda Jolly.

A sailing ship, the *Happy Harry*, blown ashore by a storm and finishing up alongside the pier in the 1950s. Since the early 1800s a very high number of ships has been lost amid the dangerous channels and sandbanks off the Southport shoreline, especially in the days of sail. The area from the entrance to the River Mersey to the River Ribble was not only very busy but also extremely hazardous.

The waste paper baling shed at the Town Lane Depot, Southport, mid-1950s. The man to the left of the centre bale is Tommy Bamber, Foreman.

'Queen' Catherine Berry being 'crowned' by the Mayoress of Southport, 1953. Reminiscent of the street parties of 1945, repeated for the 50th anniversary of VE Day, this 'street party' was actually held in the schoolyard of the County Primary School, Birkdale, to celebrate the coronation of HM Queen Elizabeth II. Among the participants were Stewart Barton, Michael and Peter Eccles, Jean Hardman, Sarah Prescott, Mary Bentham, Barbara Rimmer, Betty Brookfield, Jimmy and Brian Wallworth, Thelma Roberts, Ester and Joan Briggs, Michael Hignett, Doreen, Eunice and Audrey Rimmer, John, Alan and Elsie Kendall, Marie and Bill Howard.

The winner and runners up in Southport's 'English Rose' competition for 1954. In the centre is Mrs Jean Ferguson, who received a cheque for £850, to the left the 'Scottish Rose' and 'Midland Rose', and to the right the 'Yorkshire Rose' and 'Lancashire Rose'.

Miss Maureen Bradley, winner of the Southport 'English Rose' competition for 1955, seen here wearing her sash. The celebrity making the presentation was Arthur Askey, with daughter Anthea on the far right. The other girls in the line-up are runners up in the final.

The venue for the above photograph was The Royal Hotel, Southport, where Messrs Rushton & Co.'s Christmas dinner is about to start, late 1950s. Mr Rushton is standing, centre back, with the photograph donor, Mrs Longworth, standing right of centre.

A postcard inscribed 'wedding in Southport about 1930'.

The Sea Bathing Lake is the backdrop for this 1959 'English Rose' competition.

The 'English Rose' competition title winner, Miss Marion Lewis, at the customary venue of the Sea Bathing Lake, September 1953. She was presented with her prize by Arthur Askey, the showbusiness celebrity. There are some rather interesting faces in the crowd as well, don't you agree?

Another trio of competitors here: winner and two runners up. The winner collected prize money of £1,000 in 1961. Sadly, it has not proved possible to identify these girls.

A group of children at Norwood Road Junior School in the district of Blowick, Southport, *c.* 1965. The school was demolished during the 1980s. Among the pupils are Dianne Cornick, Carl Moon and Paul Longworth.

Messrs White and Hudson Ltd's annual children's Christmas party held here at Thorps Café, Nevill Street, December 1966.

In August 1975 teams from seven countries competed in the international television competition *It's a Knock Out*, held at the Sea Bathing Lake, Princes Park. One of the showpieces used in the event was a mock Spanish galleon complete with firing cannons. The BBC galleon, constructed at a cost of £10,000 was to be retained in Southport once the competition was over. It was estimated that some seven thousand visitors came to the town as a result of this event. The television presentation went out to an audience in Europe and in Britain, the teams taking part coming from Belgium, France, Germany, Holland, Italy, Switzerland and England. Unfortunately, the English team only managed to finish in sixth position.

In a subsequent contest, a Southport team represented England in Belgium; that team is shown above, *c.* 1977. The group includes David Rodger (extreme left), a well-known local weightlifter, who still runs a Southport gym. To the right is team manager Harry Boyle, a former football player for the Rochdale and Southport clubs; today he is a scout for premier league clubs.

Gala and fancy dress parade passing along Lord Street, mid-1950s.

Acknowledgements

Thanks for all the historical gleanings obtained, from both written and verbal sources, and for all the photographs used in the book, loaned from official and private collections. My gratitude also for the anecdotes and narratives heard during many interviews conducted in the course of my research. Thanks are due to: Sefton Metropolitan Borough Council – P. King and D. Taylor of the Department of Tourism and Leisure, Mr Swarbrick of the Community Relations Department, The Botanic Gardens Museum, the staff of Southport Library. Thanks also to the editor and staff of the *Southport Visitor*, including Mrs A. Birchall and G. Wright; the chairman and secretary of Southport and Ainsdale Golf Club; M. Connard of Messrs Connard and Son Ltd, jewellers, Lord Street; H. Highton and staff of Messrs T.R. Highton, furnishers, Lord Street; the manager and staff of Messrs Broadbents and Boothroyds, Lord Street; J. Spencer and A. Moss of Lakeside Miniature Railway; the staff of Mellors Confectioners Ltd, Butts Lane; R. Nelson of N.B. Colour Print Ltd, Chorley. My thanks to the following individuals: Mrs P. Catterall, M. Duffy, Mrs J. Freeman, Mrs D. Firgarth, A Gibbons, A. Harrison, G. Isaacs, Mrs A. Johnson, Mrs A. Longworth, W. Longton, J. Naylor, D. Nateby, Mrs J. Cooper, R. Percival, H. Soden, Mrs F. Scott, Mrs R. Taylor.

A special thank you to Barbara Kavanagh, for many happy days in Southport, especially in association with the Wayfarers Arcade.

BRITAIN IN OLD PHOTOGRAPHS

ALDERNEY

Alderney: A Second Selection, *B Bonnard*

BEDFORDSHIRE

Bedfordshire at Work, *N Lutt*

BERKSHIRE

Maidenhead, *M Hayles & D Hedges*
Around Maidenhead, *M Hayles & B Hedges*
Reading, *P Southerton*
Reading: A Second Selection, *P Southerton*
Sandhurst and Crowthorne, *K Dancy*
Around Slough, *J Hunter & K Hunter*
Around Thatcham, *P Allen*
Around Windsor, *B Hedges*

BUCKINGHAMSHIRE

Buckingham and District, *R Cook*
High Wycombe, *R Goodearl*
Around Stony Stratford, *A Lambert*

CHESHIRE

Cheshire Railways, *M Hitches*
Chester, *S Nichols*

CLWYD

Clwyd Railways, *M Hitches*

CLYDESDALE

Clydesdale, *Lesmahagow Parish Historical Association*

CORNWALL

Cornish Coast, *T Bowden*
Falmouth, *P Gilson*
Lower Fal, *P Gilson*
Around Padstow, *M McCarthy*
Around Penzance, *J Holmes*
Penzance and Newlyn, *J Holmes*
Around Truro, *A Lyne*
Upper Fal, *P Gilson*

CUMBERLAND

Cockermouth and District, *J Bernard Bradbury*
Keswick and the Central Lakes, *J Marsh*
Around Penrith, *F Boyd*
Around Whitehaven, *H Fancy*

DERBYSHIRE

Derby, *D Buxton*
Around Matlock, *D Barton*

DEVON

Colyton and Seaton, *T Gosling*
Dawlish and Teignmouth, *G Gosling*
Devon Aerodromes, *K Saunders*
Exeter, *P Thomas*
Exmouth and Budleigh Salterton, *T Gosling*
From Haldon to Mid-Dartmoor, *T Hall*
Honiton and the Otter Valley, *J Yallop*
Around Kingsbridge, *K Tanner*
Around Seaton and Sidmouth, *T Gosling*
Seaton, Axminster and Lyme Regis, *T Gosling*

DORSET

Around Blandford Forum, *B Cox*
Bournemouth, *M Colman*
Bridport and the Bride Valley, *J Burrell & S Humphries*
Dorchester, *T Gosling*
Around Gillingham, *P Crocker*

DURHAM

Darlington, *G Flynn*
Darlington: A Second Selection, *G Flynn*
Durham People, *M Richardson*
Houghton-le-Spring and Hetton-le-Hole, *K Richardson*
Houghton-le-Spring and Hetton-le-Hole: A Second Selection, *K Richardson*
Sunderland, *S Miller & B Bell*
Teesdale, *D Coggins*
Teesdale: A Second Selection, *P Raine*
Weardale, *J Crosby*
Weardale: A Second Selection, *J Crosby*

DYFED

Aberystwyth and North Ceredigion, *Dyfed Cultural Services Dept*
Haverfordwest, *Dyfed Cultural Services Dept*
Upper Tywi Valley, *Dyfed Cultural Services Dept*

ESSEX

Around Grays, *B Evans*

GLOUCESTERSHIRE

Along the Avon from Stratford to Tewkesbury, *J Jeremiah*
Cheltenham: A Second Selection, *R Whiting*
Cheltenham at War, *P Gill*
Cirencester, *J Welsford*
Around Cirencester, *E Cuss & P Griffiths*
Forest, The, *D Mullin*
Gloucester, *J Voyce*
Around Gloucester, *A Sutton*
Gloucester: From the Walwin Collection, *J Voyce*
North Cotswolds, *D Viner*
Severn Vale, *A Sutton*
Stonehouse to Painswick, *A Sutton*
Stroud and the Five Valleys, *S Gardiner & L Padin*
Stroud and the Five Valleys: A Second Selection, *S Gardiner & L Padin*
Stroud's Golden Valley, *S Gardiner & L Padin*
Stroudwater and Thames & Severn Canals, *E Cuss & S Gardiner*
Stroudwater and Thames & Severn Canals: A Second Selection, *E Cuss & S Gardiner*
Tewkesbury and the Vale of Gloucester, *C Hilton*
Thornbury to Berkeley, *J Hudson*
Uley, Dursley and Cam, *A Sutton*
Wotton-under-Edge to Chipping Sodbury, *A Sutton*

GWYNEDD

Anglesey, *M Hitches*
Gwynedd Railways, *M Hitches*
Around Llandudno, *M Hitches*
Vale of Conwy, *M Hitches*

HAMPSHIRE

Gosport, *J Sadden*
Portsmouth, *P Rogers & D Francis*

HEREFORDSHIRE

Herefordshire, *A Sandford*

HERTFORDSHIRE

Barnet, *I Norrie*
Hitchin, *A Fleck*
St Albans, *S Mullins*
Stevenage, *M Appleton*

ISLE OF MAN

The Tourist Trophy, *B Snelling*

ISLE OF WIGHT

Newport, *D Parr*
Around Ryde, *D Parr*

JERSEY

Jersey: A Third Selection, *R Lemprière*

KENT

Bexley, *M Scott*
Broadstairs and St Peter's, *J Whyman*
Bromley, Keston and Hayes, *M Scott*
Canterbury: A Second Selection, *D Butler*
Chatham and Gillingham, *P MacDougall*
Chatham Dockyard, *P MacDougall*
Deal, *J Broady*
Early Broadstairs and St Peter's, *B Wootton*
East Kent at War, *D Collyer*
Eltham, *J Kennett*
Folkestone: A Second Selection, *A Taylor & E Rooney*
Goudhurst to Tenterden, *A Guilmant*
Gravesend, *R Hiscock*
Around Gravesham, *R Hiscock & D Grierson*
Herne Bay, *J Hawkins*
Lympne Airport, *D Collyer*
Maidstone, *I Hales*
Margate, *R Clements*
RAF Hawkinge, *R Humphreys*
RAF Manston, *RAF Manston History Club*
RAF Manston: A Second Selection, *RAF Manston History Club*
Ramsgate and Thanet Life, *D Perkins*
Romney Marsh, *E Carpenter*
Sandwich, *C Wanostrocht*
Around Tonbridge, *C Bell*
Tunbridge Wells, *M Rowlands & I Beavis*
Tunbridge Wells: A Second Selection, *M Rowlands & I Beavis*
Around Whitstable, *C Court*
Wingham, Adisham and Littlebourne, *M Crane*

LANCASHIRE

Around Barrow-in-Furness, *J Garbutt & J Marsh*
Blackpool, *C Rothwell*
Bury, *J Hudson*
Chorley and District, *J Smith*
Fleetwood, *C Rothwell*
Heywood, *J Hudson*
Around Kirkham, *C Rothwell*
Lancashire North of the Sands, *J Garbutt & J Marsh*
Around Lancaster, *S Ashworth*
Lytham St Anne's, *C Rothwell*
North Fylde, *C Rothwell*
Radcliffe, *J Hudson*
Rossendale, *B Moore & N Dunnachie*

LEICESTERSHIRE

Around Ashby-de-la-Zouch, *K Hillier*
Charnwood Forest, *I Keil, W Humphrey & D Wix*
Leicester, *D Burton*
Leicester: A Second Selection, *D Burton*
Melton Mowbray, *T Hickman*
Around Melton Mowbray, *T Hickman*
River Soar, *D Wix, P Shacklock & I Keil*
Rutland, *T Clough*
Vale of Belvoir, *T Hickman*
Around the Welland Valley, *S Mastoris*

LINCOLNSHIRE

Grimsby, *J Tierney*
Around Grimsby, *J Tierney*
Grimsby Docks, *J Tierney*
Lincoln, *D Cuppleditch*

Scunthorpe, *D Taylor*
Skegness, *W Kime*
Around Skegness, *W Kime*

LONDON

Balham and Tooting, *P Loobey*
Crystal Palace, Penge & Anerley, *M Scott*
Greenwich and Woolwich, *K Clark*
Hackney: A Second Selection, *D Mander*
Lewisham and Deptford, *J Coulter*
Lewisham and Deptford: A Second Selection, *J Coulter*
Streatham, *P Loobey*
Around Whetstone and North Finchley, *J Heathfield*
Woolwich, *B Evans*

MONMOUTHSHIRE

Chepstow and the River Wye, *A Rainsbury*
Monmouth and the River Wye, *Monmouth Museum*

NORFOLK

Great Yarmouth, *M Teun*
Norwich, *M Colman*
Wymondham and Attleborough, *P Yaxley*

NORTHAMPTONSHIRE

Around Stony Stratford, *A Lambert*

NOTTINGHAMSHIRE

Arnold and Bestwood, *M Spick*
Arnold and Bestwood: A Second Selection, *M Spick*
Changing Face of Nottingham, *G Oldfield*
Mansfield, *Old Mansfield Society*
Around Newark, *T Warner*
Nottingham: 1944–1974, *D Whitworth*
Sherwood Forest, *D Ottewell*
Victorian Nottingham, *M Payne*

OXFORDSHIRE

Around Abingdon, *P Horn*
Banburyshire, *M Barnett & S Gosling*
Burford, *A Jewell*
Around Didcot and the Hagbournes, *B Lingham*
Garsington, *M Gunther*
Around Henley-on-Thames, *S Ellis*
Oxford: The University, *J Rhodes*
Thame to Watlington, *N Hood*
Around Wallingford, *D Beasley*
Witney, *T Worley*
Around Witney, *C Mitchell*
Witney District, *T Worley*
Around Woodstock, *J Bond*

POWYS

Brecon, *Brecknock Museum*
Welshpool, *E Bredsdorff*

SHROPSHIRE

Shrewsbury, *D Trumper*
Whitchurch to Market Drayton, *M Morris*

SOMERSET

Bath, *J Hudson*
Bridgwater and the River Parrett, *R Fitzhugh*
Bristol, *D Moorcroft & N Campbell-Sharp*
Changing Face of Keynsham,
B Lowe & M Whitehead
Chard and Ilminster, *G Gosling & F Huddy*
Crewkerne and the Ham Stone Villages,
G Gosling & F Huddy
Around Keynsham and Saltford, *B Lowe & T Brown*
Midsomer Norton and Radstock, *C Howell*
Somerton, Ilchester and Langport, *G Gosling & F Huddy*
Taunton, *N Chipchase*
Around Taunton, *N Chipchase*
Wells, *C Howell*
Weston-Super-Mare, *S Poole*
Around Weston-Super-Mare, *S Poole*
West Somerset Villages, *K Houghton & L Thomas*

STAFFORDSHIRE

Aldridge, *J Farrow*
Bilston, *E Rees*
Black Country Transport: Aviation, *A Brew*
Around Burton upon Trent, *G Sowerby & R Farman*
Bushbury, *A Chatwin, M Mills & E Rees*
Around Cannock, *M Mills & S Belcher*
Around Leek, *R Poole*
Lichfield, *H Clayton & K Simmons*
Around Pattingham and Wombourne, *M Griffiths, P Leigh & M Mills*
Around Rugeley, *T Randall & J Anslow*
Smethwick, *J Maddison*
Stafford, *J Anslow & T Randall*
Around Stafford, *J Anslow & T Randall*
Stoke-on-Trent, *I Lawley*
Around Tamworth, *R Sulima*
Around Tettenhall and Codsall, *M Mills*
Tipton, Wednesbury and Darlaston, *R Pearson*
Walsall, *D Gilbert & M Lewis*
Wednesbury, *I Bott*
West Bromwich, *R Pearson*

SUFFOLK

Ipswich: A Second Selection, *D Kindred*
Around Ipswich, *D Kindred*
Around Mildenhall, *C Dring*
Southwold to Aldeburgh, *H Phelps*
Around Woodbridge, *H Phelps*

SURREY

Cheam and Belmont, *P Berry*
Croydon, *S Bligh*
Dorking and District, *K Harding*
Around Dorking, *A Jackson*
Around Epsom, *P Berry*
Farnham: A Second Selection, *J Parratt*
Around Haslemere and Hindhead, *T Winter & G Collyer*
Richmond, *Richmond Local History Society*
Sutton, *P Berry*

SUSSEX

Arundel and the Arun Valley, *J Godfrey*
Bishopstone and Seaford, *P Pople & P Berry*
Brighton and Hove, *J Middleton*
Brighton and Hove: A Second Selection, *J Middleton*
Around Crawley, *M Goldsmith*
Hastings, *P Haines*
Hastings: A Second Selection, *P Haines*
Around Haywards Heath, *J Middleton*
Around Heathfield, *A Gillet & B Russell*
Around Heathfield: A Second Selection,
A Gillet & B Russell
High Weald, *B Harwood*
High Weald: A Second Selection, *B Harwood*
Horsham and District, *T Wales*
Lewes, *J Middleton*
RAF Tangmere, *A Saunders*
Around Rye, *A Dickinson*
Around Worthing, *S White*

WARWICKSHIRE

Along the Avon from Stratford to Tewkesbury, *J Jeremiah*
Bedworth, *J Burton*
Coventry, *D McGrory*
Around Coventry, *D McGrory*
Nuneaton, *S Clews & S Vaughan*
Around Royal Leamington Spa, *J Cameron*
Around Royal Leamington Spa: A Second Selection,
J Cameron
Around Warwick, *R Booth*

WESTMORLAND

Eden Valley, *J Marsh*
Kendal, *M & P Duff*
South Westmorland Villages, *J Marsh*
Westmorland Lakes, *J Marsh*

WILTSHIRE

Around Amesbury, *P Daniels*
Chippenham and Lacock, *A Wilson & M Wilson*
Around Corsham and Box, *A Wilson & M Wilson*
Around Devizes, *D Buxton*
Around Highworth, *G Tanner*
Around Highworth and Faringdon, *G Tanner*
Around Malmesbury, *A Wilson*
Marlborough: A Second Selection, *P Colman*
Around Melksham,
Melksham and District Historical Association
Nadder Valley, *R. Sawyer*
Salisbury, *P Saunders*
Salisbury: A Second Selection, *P Daniels*
Salisbury: A Third Selection, *P Daniels*
Around Salisbury, *P Daniels*
Swindon: A Third Selection, *The Swindon Society*
Swindon: A Fourth Selection, *The Swindon Society*
Trowbridge, *M Marshman*
Around Wilton, *P Daniels*
Around Wootton Bassett, Cricklade and Purton, *T Sharp*

WORCESTERSHIRE

Evesham to Bredon, *F Archer*
Around Malvern, *K Smith*
Around Pershore, *M Dowty*
Redditch and the Needle District, *R Saunders*
Redditch: A Second Selection, *R Saunders*
Around Tenbury Wells, *D Green*
Worcester, *M Dowty*
Around Worcester, *R Jones*
Worcester in a Day, *M Dowty*
Worcestershire at Work, *R Jones*

YORKSHIRE

Huddersfield: A Second Selection, *H Wheeler*
Huddersfield: A Third Selection, *H Wheeler*
Leeds Road and Rail, *R Vickers*
Pontefract, *R van Riel*
Scarborough, *D Coggins*
Scarborough's War Years, *R Percy*
Skipton and the Dales, *Friends of the Craven Museum*
Around Skipton-in-Craven, *Friends of the Craven Museum*
Yorkshire Wolds, *I & M Sumner*